TERRIFIC TOYS

TERRIFIC TOYS FROM AROUND THE WORLD

By Noah Leatherland

KidHaven PUBLISHING

Published in 2025 by
KidHaven Publishing, an Imprint of Greenhaven Publishing, LLC
2544 Clinton St., Buffalo, NY 14224

Written by: Noah Leatherland
Edited by: Rebecca Phillips-Bartlett
Designed by: Amelia Harris

Cataloging-in-Publication Data

Names: Leatherland, Noah, 1999-.
Title: Terrific toys from around the world / Noah Leatherland.
Description: Buffalo, New York : KidHaven Publishing, 2025. | Series: Terrific toys | Includes glossary and index.
Identifiers: ISBN 9781534547162 (pbk.) | ISBN 9781534547179 (library bound) | ISBN 9781534547186 (ebook)
Subjects: LCSH: Toys--Juvenile literature. | Toys--Social aspects--Juvenile literature.
Classification: LCC GV1218.5 L438 2025 | DDC 649'.55--dc23

Manufactured in the United States of America

CPSIA compliance information: Batch #CSKH25: For further information contact Greenhaven Publishing LLC at 1-844-317-7404.

Please visit our website, www.greenhavenpublishing.com.
For a free color catalog of all our high-quality books, call toll free 1-844-317-7404 or fax 1-844-317-7405.

Find us on

Image Credits

All images are courtesy of Shutterstock.com, unless otherwise specified. With thanks to Getty Images, Thinkstock Photo and iStockphoto. Cover – Mauro Rodrigues, anaken2012, Alfa Photostudio, Noel V. Baebler. Used on all pages – Shmelkova Nataliya. 4 – New Africa. 5 – StockImageFactory.com, engagestock. 6&7 – Pamela Toledo. 8 – Kanizuki, DigitalStock. 9 – Mirko Kuzmanovic, Serhii Ivashchuk. 10&11 – Ezume Images. 11 – Eric Valenne geostory. 12 – Anne Marlene Arkwright, duckeesue. 13 – Dani Simmonds, claire norman. 14 – fpdress. 14&15 – Rizvisual. 16 – Lucian Coman. 17 – Anke van Wyk. 18&19 – Manu Verdier. 19 – Serge73. 20 – Rawpixel.com, Sergey Novikov. 21 – Twinsterphoto. 22 – kai keisuke, Lost in the past, Elzbieta Sekowska. 23 – EQRoy, Cris_mh.

Contents

Words that look like **this** can be found in the glossary on page 24.

A World of Toys

From rapid race cars to cuddly teddy bears, people have come up with all sorts of toys. All around the world, there are millions of terrific toys to play with. Think of all the fun!

What is your favorite toy?

The toys you play with might be different from what children in other parts of the world play with. Some toys are **traditional** in certain places and have been around for many years.

Chile

In Chile, there is a game called *emboque*. It is a traditional game. It uses a wooden stick and cap joined together with a piece of string.

Would you be able to catch the cap?

The player holds the stick and flicks the cap into the air. Then they have to try to catch the cap on the end of the stick. It can be really tricky!

China

In China, lots of people play with a toy called a *jianzi*. A jianzi is a rubber top with feathers attached, a bit like a shuttlecock. The feathers can be all sorts of colors.

Shuttlecock

The goal is to kick the jianzi and keep it up in the air.

Players can play by themselves or find another player and kick it over a net.

Ghana

Oware is a board game found all over Africa. There are lots of different **varieties** of the game. Oware is thought to have first been made in Ghana. The board might look different in other countries.

Oware is played by two people. Players try to win the game by collecting the most seeds on the board. The game is also used to help children learn to count.

The seeds can be made of stone or glass. Sometimes players use real seeds!

Guatemala

Guatemalan worry dolls are very small. Sometimes they are only around 1 inch (2.5 cm) tall.

They are made of wood or wire and fabric. Worry dolls are dressed in traditional Guatemalan clothes.

Worry dolls are said to help people with their worries.

People say that if you tell the doll what you are worried about and put it under your pillow, you will feel much better in the morning.

Japan

Daruma Otoshi is a traditional Japanese game. It is played with a **stack** of wooden blocks and a small hammer.

The top wooden block has a face painted on it.

Players use the hammer to hit the pieces out of the stack without the rest falling over. The goal is to have just the face left standing.

Do not hit the block in the face!

Malawi

In Malawi, lots of children play with *galimotos*. "Galimoto" means "car" in the Chichewa language. Galimoto toys are pushed around with sticks.

Galimotos are made from **recycled** objects. They are often made from metal and wire. Most of the time, children make galimoto toys themselves.

Have you ever made your own toys?

Mexico

Maria dolls are soft toys made in Mexico. The dolls have braided hair with ribbons. Their dresses are made from colorful fabrics. They are often handmade by street vendors.

Some people believe that Maria dolls help protect children from evil spirits.

Maria dolls are often given as gifts to keep people safe.

Why Are Our Toys Different?

Toys are not the only things that are different all over the world.

Different places have their own foods, clothes, languages, and traditions.

Toys are an important part of each country's culture. Looking at terrific toys from around the world can teach us about different people and their cultures.

What toys from around the world would you want to play with?

Fun Facts

Spinning top toys have been found in Egyptian **tombs** from thousands of years ago.

Different cultures have made similar toys without realizing it.

A doll from Bulgaria

A doll from Eswatini

In Rochester, New York, there is a Toy Hall of Fame where you can see toys from all over the world!

Many of your toys might have been made in another country.

Glossary

culture the traditions, ideas, and ways of life of a group of people

recycled used again to make something else

spirits beings that are not part of this world, such as a ghost or devil

stack a pile of objects, especially one that is neatly arranged

tombs large structures or rooms for burying the dead

traditional describing something that is passed down between people over time

varieties different types of similar things

vendors people who sell things

Index